JANE GOODALL'S ANIMAL WORLD

SEA OTTERS

by Ruth Ashby

Scientific Consultant: Friends of the Sea Otter

A Byron Preiss Book

Atheneum   1990   New York

◇ Introduction: The Sea Otter by Jane Goodall

I shall never forget the morning I spent watching sea otters from a small boat off the California coast. It was a visit to an enchanted world peopled by round-faced, beady-eyed, thick-furred denizens of the open seas. I was with Margaret Owings, one of the best friends the sea otters have ever had.

It was a calm day, and once we had reached the great kelp bed, we let the boat drift among the brown fronds of seaweed that moved with the waves. After about fifteen minutes we saw the first head pop up from the water. Two bright, inquisitive eyes gazed at us intently, and then the otter relaxed.

He stayed on the surface a while, lolling on his back with his brown furry tummy exposed to the morning sun, his front paws folded on his chest. And then, with a lightning movement, he rolled over and dived from sight. "There he is!" said Margaret a minute later. This time the otter was holding a little crab on his chest. With smacking sounds he dismembered the crustacean and crunched up the flesh. His chest, by the end of the snack, was covered with bits of shell. And then he was gone.

At that moment another otter bobbed into sight. To my delight he began to bang open a big shellfish, hitting it against a rock that he had brought up from the ocean floor and placed on his chest. He was using the rock as a tool. Bang! Bang! Bang! And the shell cracked. In my mind's eye I can still see his bewhiskered face eating the delicious snack.

Margaret Owings told me how she had first become interested in the otters when she moved to live in a house overlooking the ocean. At that time, in the 1960s, the few otters that had survived the fur trade of the previous century were being threatened by the abalone fishermen, who maintained they ate too many of these big shellfish and hurt their livelihood.

Margaret Owings believed that the sea otters had as much right to their share of the ocean's bounty as the fishermen. She founded an organization, Friends of the Sea Otter, which began the fight to save the otters. That is a very wonderful story, not only because it preserved a fascinating and truly delightful species from probable extinction, but also because it shows how one determined person can make a difference. That is a lesson we all should learn.

◇ Contents

◇ Where Do Sea Otters Live?

Sea otters are found along the North Pacific Coast, from central California, Alaska, and the Aleutian Islands in the United States to Kamchatka and the Kuril Islands in the Soviet Union. As their name suggests, sea otters live mainly in the ocean and hardly ever go ashore. Sea otters who live in the colder waters off Alaska may go up on land more often than do California otters, because it is warmer onshore.

Sea otters make their home in kelp beds, floating islands of seaweed that are attached to rocks at the bottom of the sea. In the kelp they eat, play, sleep, and groom—nearly everything but mate and hunt for food. To find the shellfish that are their main diet, they must dive down to the bottom of the ocean.

Other aquatic mammals such as seals and sea lions also swim around the kelp beds with the sea otters. A long-necked bird called the cormorant glides through the kelp forests, catching fish underwater.

The sea otter has natural enemies too. Bald eagles sometimes carry off sea otter pups, especially to feed their young. And the white shark, Greenland shark, and killer whale also have been known to attack sea otters.

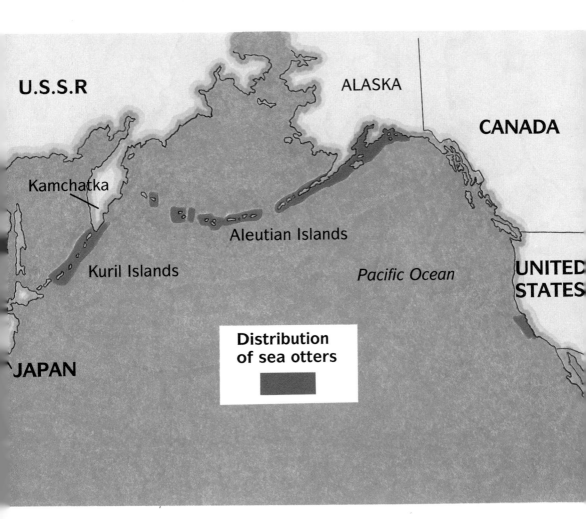

U.S.S.R

ALASKA

CANADA

Kamchatka

Aleutian Islands

Kuril Islands

Pacific Ocean

UNITED STATES

JAPAN

Distribution of sea otters

◇ The Family Tree of the Sea Otter

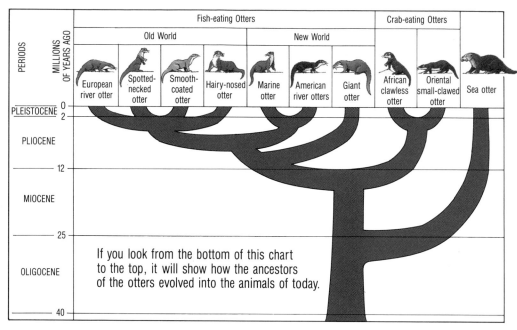

		Fish-eating Otters						Crab-eating Otters		

This family tree is based on the best available information about otter evolution, which scientists are still studying.

Sea otters *(Enhydra lutris)* (in-*hi*-drah *loo*-triss) are mammals and members of the weasel family, called *Mustelidae* (muss-*tell*-uh-dee). Mustelids are medium-sized to small meat-eaters, with long, slender bodies and short legs. Other mustelids are the mink, skunk, badger, and polecat, and of course, other otters.

There are twelve species of otters altogether, including river otters, the African clawless otter, the Asian small-clawed otter, the spotted-necked otter, the smooth-coated otter, the marine otter, and the giant otter. Some scientists think there are even two subspecies of sea otters, the California and Alaska, because the two kinds are different in behavior and the bones in their skulls are different. All otters live in or near water, generally

The flipperlike feet of the sea otter

rivers, lakes, or streams, but only the sea otter and marine otter live mainly in the ocean.

The ancestors of all otters were probably land-dwellers who learned to hunt for fish and other aquatic creatures. As they evolved, they adapted to life in the water. Today otters have webbed feet and teeth that are specially shaped for crushing shells or slicing fish.

A yawning sea otter shows its teeth.

◇ The Sea Otter Community

Sea otters are often solitary but they rest and socialize in large groups called *rafts*. Rafts can consist of only three or four to a few hundred sea otters. Once 2,000 sea otters were seen rafting together. Rafts are usually all-male or all-female. The all-female rafts include mothers and their young pups. This family group is the most basic unit of sea otter life. Males do not help the females to raise the young.

Individual sea otters have home areas or *ranges* in which they rest and hunt for food. These ranges overlap considerably with those of other otters. Ordinarily, sea otters do not defend these ranges against their neighbors.

Some adult males do, however, establish ranges that they defend against other males. These are called *territories* and are in areas where many females live. When other males come into these territories, they are chased away. Sometimes two males will even fight.

No one is quite sure why some males are territorial and others aren't. It is possible that males who have their own territories can court and mate with a female with less competition from other males. Territorial males get the chance to mate with females who swim through their territories or come there to feed.

◇ Sizing Up the Sea Otter

Sea otters are the largest of all the otters and the largest members of the weasel family. On average, a male weighs sixty-two pounds and reaches a length of just over four feet, including tail. The average female weighs forty-five pounds and is just under four feet long.

The biggest male sea otters can weigh up to one hundred pounds.

Sea otter
4 feet

River otter
2½ feet

Badger
2 feet

Skunk
15 inches

Mink
14 inches

◇ How the Sea Otter Moves

Sea otters swim underwater by moving their tails and their large, webbed, hind feet up and down at the same time. When they are swimming on the surface, they usually lie on their backs and keep their heads and shoulders out of the water while they kick with their flippers. Sea otters are somewhat clumsy on land and cannot move very quickly.

In order to eat, sea otters must dive to find food. Because they are mammals and need air to breathe, they can stay under

for only short periods of time. Generally, dives last between fifty and ninety seconds, though when sea otters are in danger they can remain underwater for as long as four minutes.

Sea otters rest on the surface of the water. They lie on their backs with their heads up and their feet out of the water. This is where they are most comfortable. So they won't float away, they often wrap themselves in strands of kelp that are anchored to the bottom of the ocean.

◇ The Senses of the Sea Otter

The sea otters' senses are adapted for life in the sea. Their ears are small and round and close when they are underwater. So do their nostrils. Since sea otters cannot smell or hear prey when they are hunting, they depend a great deal on their sight and sense of touch.

The sea otter's eyes are rounder than those of humans. This shape allows light to enter at a different angle, so that sea otters have better vision underwater than we do.

However, they probably rely more on touch than on sight to find food. Their front paws are sensitive and dexterous, and their whiskers are also responsive to touch. When sea otters dive to the ocean floor to hunt, the water is often dark or murky. They must find food by feeling for it. They can tell a mussel from an abalone simply by touch.

They bring their prey to the surface in order to eat it. If the prey has a hard shell, otters use a tool to crack it open. They put a rock on their chests and bang the shellfish against it.

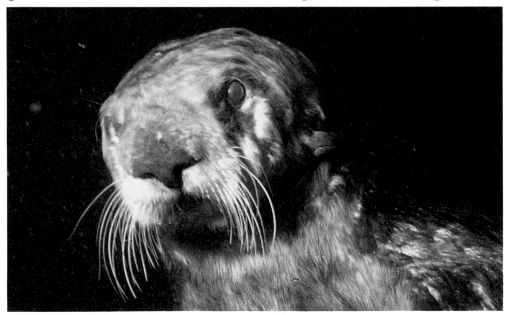

A sea otter keeps its eyes open underwater.

A sea otter grooms its fur.

Sea otters are the only mammals besides chimpanzees and humans who use tools regularly in their daily lives. Many creatures use tools occasionally, especially elephants.

The sea otter has the thickest fur of any mammal—there are about 700,000 hairs in every square inch! Its coat has two layers, a top layer of long hair and an undercoat of thick fur. The long hair is waterproof, and the underfur traps a layer of air. This air insulates sea otters from the cold water. Unlike seals and whales, sea otters do not have a layer of blubber, so they rely on this cushion of air to keep them warm.

In order to keep their fur waterproof, sea otters spend a lot of time grooming. They trap air in their fur by blowing into it and by splashing the water around them into a bubbly froth.

The air bubbles in their fur also help sea otters to float.

16

◇ How Sea Otters Communicate

Most otters communicate through scent-marking. They leave deposits of dung, or *spraint*, on the ground. The spraint allows the next otters who pass by to identify the individual who left it.

Because sea otters live in the water, their dung washes away and smells disappear rapidly. Sea otters can identify each other by smell only at close range. For instance, a male looking for a partner will cruise around a group of females. He can tell whether a female is ready to mate by her smell.

Sea otters also communicate by sound. When otters are slightly distressed they make a loud whistling sound. A growl or a hiss acts as a threat. When very upset, sea otters let out high-pitched, ear-piercing screams. Contented sea otters grunt and "coo."

Another way sea otters communicate is through body language. Otters often swing their heads from side to side when greeting other otters.

◇ Being Born

Courting sea otters play together.

Sea otters can mate any time of the year. When they are courting, sea otters "play" together. They chase each other, swimming and diving through the water. Courting lasts for two to four days. When sea otters mate, the male bites the female's nose. Many females have badly scarred noses.

Baby sea otters may be born four to six months later. The mother gives birth to only one pup at a time, usually in the

water but sometimes on the beach. The first thing the mother does is groom the pup so its fur is dry and fluffy. She keeps it on her stomach until its fur has enough air bubbles to allow the pup to float by itself. Only then can she groom herself or search for food.

◇ Growing Up

A sea otter pup depends on its mother for everything during the first months of its life. Pups continue to drink their mothers' milk for six to eight months in California and for up to a year in Alaska. When the pup is two months old, it can eat solid foods as well, and it shares the spoils of its mother's hunting. Gradually the pup learns how to find shellfish for itself.

From its mother the youngster also learns how to use a rock as a tool to smash shellfish and get at the meat inside.

The most important thing a young sea otter has to learn is how to swim and dive. Soon after it is born, it can float and swim a little. But it needs practice to learn how to dive. The trapped air bubbles in its fur make it difficult for the pup to get all the way down to the bottom of the ocean, where the

shellfish are. As it becomes stronger, it is able to dive deeper and stay down for a longer time.

The bond between mother and pup gradually weakens as the youngster becomes increasingly independent. By the time it is about one year old, it is ready to live on its own.

Female sea otters can give birth by the time they are about three or four years of age. Sea otters can live to be about fifteen years old.

◇ Living Day to Day

It is early morning in Monterey Bay, California. In the middle of an all-female raft, a mother sea otter and her pup float in a bed of kelp. The mother begins to groom her youngster. The pup stays on her chest as she vigorously fluffs its fur with her forepaws. That done, she wraps the pup in some kelp and spends ten minutes grooming herself.

It is time to eat. A sea otter has a high metabolism, which

means it burns the energy from its food very quickly. In one day, it can eat one quarter of its weight in food. Most sea otters eat ten to fifteen pounds of food a day. An adult human eats only about four pounds of food in the same period of time.

The mother sea otter dives down to the bottom of the ocean. In the waters off California, the sea otter can find shellfish, sea urchins, abalone, and crabs. In Monterey Bay, they can find another speciality as well—tinned octopus. Small octopi move into old soda and beer cans that people have thrown overboard. Sea otters find the cans and tear them open to get at the octopi within.

Today, when the mother sea otter reaches the ocean floor she feels around the boulders until she finds a rock that she tucks into the flap of loose skin under her forelimb. Then she scoops up a few clams and brings them to the surface.

There she rolls over onto her back, takes out the rock, and places it on her chest. One at a time, she bangs the clams against the rock until they break open. Then she scoops out the tender meat and eats it. The pup floating by her side gets his share of the food as well.

By the time the mother sea otter has finished her meal, her chest is covered with scraps of food. When she brushes them off, nearby sea gulls swoop down to grab the leftovers that go floating by.

Still hungry, the female takes another dive. This time she finds a purple sea urchin between two rocks. Sea urchins are one of sea otters' favorite foods. After bringing the urchin to the surface, she rubs it between her paws, breaking off the spines before biting into it.

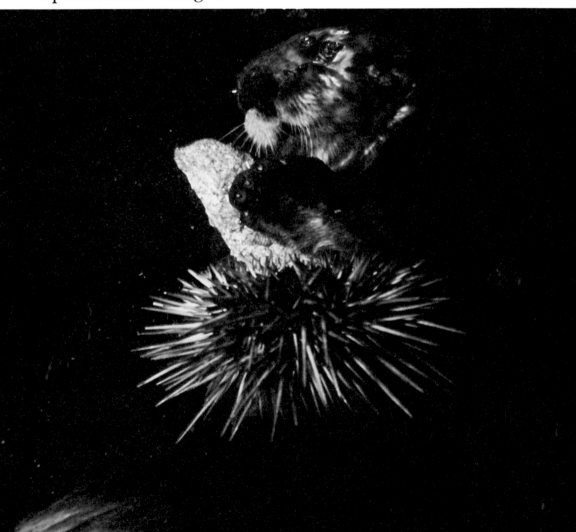

After every meal, the female must groom herself again. Sea otters must keep themselves very clean. They spend from ten to twelve percent of their time grooming.

Most of a sea otter's day is spent hunting, grooming, eating, and resting. Sea otters don't sleep for long periods of time. Instead, they take lots of short naps throughout the day and night.

Though other otters are nearby, the mother and pup seldom interact with them. Sometimes the pup swims around its mother and even tries a few short dives. It plays with a neighboring pup, and they chase each other through the waves. Occasionally a male sea otter swims by, looking for females who are in condition to mate. But this mother sea otter is not ready.

When the sun goes down over the bay, the pup is snuggled on its mother's chest. Many months will go by before it is ready to live on its own.

◇ Sea Otters in Captivity

People love to watch sea otters as they swim, play, dive, groom themselves, and paddle around on their backs in the water. But sea otters don't always do well in captivity. Aquariums must provide them with an environment that is very much like their own. Their most important needs are for clean water and plenty of food.

As we have seen, grooming is a very important part of sea otter health. If a sea otter's coat is uncared for, it won't hold the air layer that keeps the animal warm. As a result, the sea otter becomes chilled or can catch pneumonia and die. Even transporting sea otters in a crate can be dangerous. While in the crate, they don't groom themselves, and when they are released, their fur can't protect them from the cold water.

In captivity otters play more and eat less than they do in the wild. This is because they no longer have to hunt for their food at the bottom of the sea. Everything is provided for them and they have extra time and energy.

◇ Protecting the Sea Otters

In the eighteenth and nineteenth centuries, sea otter fur was more valuable than that of beavers, bison, or river otters. In the 170 years before 1911, approximately 900,000 sea otters were killed along the Alaskan coast, and 100,000 to 200,000 along the coasts of California and Mexico.

In 1911, many nations signed an agreement to stop hunting sea otters. At that time there were fewer than fifty sea otters left along the Californian coast.

Today, in a remarkable recovery, the population of California sea otters has risen to 1,864. Alaska sea otters now number between 100,000 and 150,000. This is one of the greatest success stories in the history of animal conservation.

Sea otters still face dangers from humans, however. The oceans are polluted with chemicals and wastes. In the 1970s, nearly 100 California sea otters drowned in fishing nets each year. Some otters still die in nets, but new laws have forced the fishermen to put their nets in areas where there are few otters.

The greatest danger, though, comes from oil spills. When sea otters are covered with oil, their fur does not keep them warm and they soon freeze to death. Those who do not freeze

An oil-covered sea otter comes out of the water.

A rescue team washes off an oily otter after the Valdez oil spill.

immediately can be poisoned by breathing the oil fumes and by oil they swallow when grooming or feeding. This oil destroys their kidneys, lungs, and intestinal systems.

Most otters live in waters that are the routes for huge oil tankers. When the Exxon tanker Valdez went aground off Prince William Sound in Alaska in March 1989, the oil spill killed tens of thousands of birds and sea otters. More than a thousand sea otter bodies were found, but scientists estimate that thousands more may have been killed. Many more bodies sink to the bottom of the ocean than drift up on shore where they can be counted.

If an oil spill this large had occurred off California, it might have killed all of the California sea otters. To prevent such a disaster, the U.S. Fish and Wildlife Service is trying to set up a second colony of sea otters at an offshore island many miles from the mainland range. So far, many of the otters that have been taken to the island have been reluctant to stay there. Some have managed to swim the 200 miles back to their original homes along the California coast.

Other actions to protect California sea otters from oil spills include making oil tankers travel many miles off the coast, preventing oil drilling along the sea otter's range, and building a sea otter's rescue center to care for them in case a spill occurs. We could also conserve energy so we do not need to use so much oil.

The sea otters were saved once. We have to be sure they don't run the risk of extinction again.

About the Contributors

JANE GOODALL was born in London on April 3, 1934, and grew up in Bournemouth, on the southern coast of England. In 1960, she began studying chimpanzees in the wild in Gombe, Tanzania. After receiving her doctorate in ethology at Cambridge University, Dr. Goodall founded the Gombe Stream Research Center for the study of chimpanzees and baboons. In 1977, she established the Jane Goodall Institute for Wildlife Research, Education and Conservation to promote animal research throughout the world. She has written three books for adults, including the bestseller *In the Shadow of Man*, and three books for children, including the acclaimed *My Life With the Chimpanzees* and *The Chimpanzee Family Book*.

RUTH ASHBY is an editor and teacher, and the author of two other books for children, Time Machine #23: *Quest for King Arthur*, and *Tigers*.

FRIENDS OF THE SEA OTTER is a non-profit organization dedicated to the protection of the threatened southern sea otter and its marine habitat along the central California coast. Founded in 1968, FSO strives to maintain a sound sea otter conservation program by gathering and evaluating scientific information, by monitoring activities affecting sea otters and their habitat, and by conducting educational programs, including semi-annual publication of *The Otter Raft*. To join FSO in protecting the southern sea otter, write to: Friends of the Sea Otter, P.O. Box 221220, Carmel, CA 93922.

Jane Goodall's commitment to the animal world is expressed in her words, "Only when we understand can we care. Only when we care can we help. Only when we help shall they be saved." You can learn more about joining in her efforts to protect endangered wildlife by contacting The Jane Goodall Institute for Wildlife Research, Education and Conservation, P.O. Box 26846, Tucson, Arizona 85726.

Atheneum
Macmillan Publishing Company
866 Third Avenue, New York, NY 10022
Collier Macmillan Canada, Inc.

First Edition

Printed in the United States of America

10 9 8 7 6 5 4 3 2 1

Cover photo copyright © by Tom and Pat Leeson
Back cover photo copyright © by Tom and Pat Leeson
Front cover photo insert of Jane Goodall by Hugo Van Lawick copyright © National Geographic Society
Introduction photo of Jane Goodall copyright © Ben Asen
Interior illustrations copyright © 1990 by Byron Preiss Visual Publications, Inc.

Interior photos: Pages 1, 7 (bottom), 9, 13, 15, 16, 18, 20, 24, 25, and 28 copyright © Tom and Pat Leeson; pages 7 (top), 8, 12, 14, 17, 18–19, 21, 23, 26, and 27 copyright © Jeff Foott; pages 11, 22, and 31 copyright © Len Rue, Jr.; page 29 copyright © Kathy Dawson; page 30 copyright © Tony Dawson; page 4 copyright © Tyler Gearhart/Envision.

Interior illustrations by Ralph Reese

Special thanks to Dr. Susan Shane, Margaret Owings, Judy Wilson, Jonathan Lanman, and Ana Cerro.

Editor: Ruth Ashby
Associate Editor: Gillian Bucky
Cover design: Ted Mader & Associates
Interior design: Alex Jay/Studio J

Library of Congress Cataloging-in-Publication Data
Ashby, Ruth.
    Jane Goodall's animal world. Sea otters/by Ruth Ashby.
    —1st ed.   p.   cm.
    "A Byron Preiss book."
    Summary: An introduction to sea otters, aquatic mammals that live in the north Pacific and rarely come to land.
    ISBN 0-689-31472-8
    1. Sea otter—Juvenile literature. [1. Sea otter.] I. Title.
    QL737.C25A84   1990   599.74'447—dc20
    89-38552   CIP   AC